I0800713

THE ATLANTIC OCEAN

BY JUNIATA ROGERS

The Child's World
childsworld.com

Published by The Child's World®
1980 Lookout Drive • Mankato, MN 56003-1705
800-599-READ • www.childsworld.com

Credits: Andrei Pogrebnoi/Shutterstock.com: 21; Creative icon styles: 5 (compass); holbox/Shutterstock.com: 6; lavizzara/Shutterstock.com: 10; Matt9122/Shutterstock.com: 9; Natursports/Shutterstock.com: cover, 1; NOAA/NOAA.gov: 17; Nora Yusuf/Shutterstock.com: 13; wildestanimal/Shutterstock.com:18

Copyright ©2019 by The Child's World®
All rights reserved. No part of this book may be reproduced or utilized in any form or by any means without written permission from the publisher.

ISBN HARDCOVER: 9781503825024
ISBN PAPERBACK: 9781622434343
LCCN: 2017960228

Printed in the United States of America
PA02373

TABLE OF CONTENTS

WHERE IN THE WORLD?

Look at the map. Where is the Atlantic Ocean? Can you find North and South America? They are to the west. Now find Europe. It is to the east. Africa is below Europe. The Atlantic Ocean is in the middle.

The Atlantic covers a fifth of Earth.

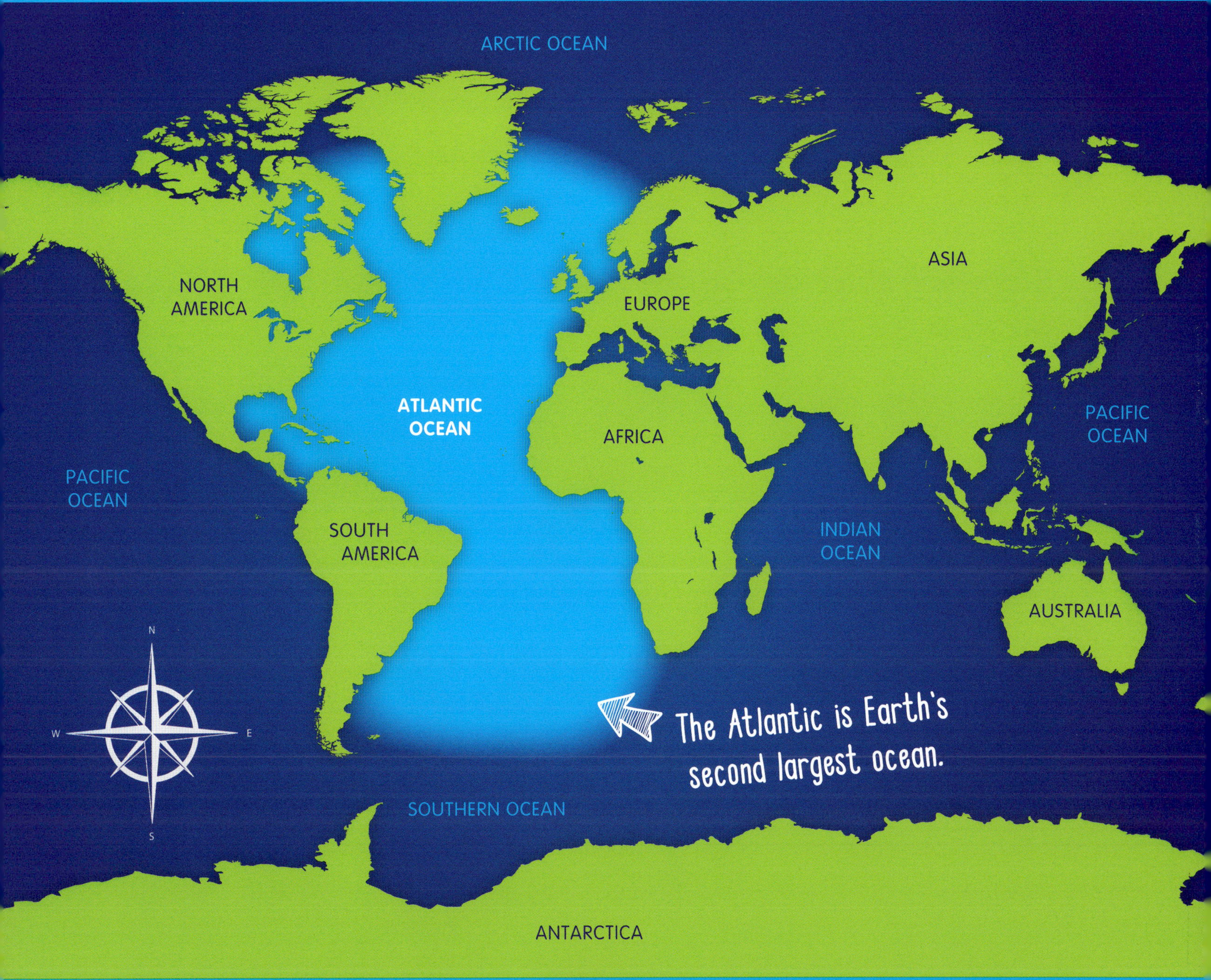
ARCTIC OCEAN
NORTH AMERICA
EUROPE
ASIA
ATLANTIC OCEAN
AFRICA
PACIFIC OCEAN
PACIFIC OCEAN
SOUTH AMERICA
INDIAN OCEAN
AUSTRALIA
N
W
E
S
The Atlantic is Earth's second largest ocean.
SOUTHERN OCEAN
ANTARCTICA

Fishermen know blue marlin follow the warm waters of the Gulf Stream.

GO WITH THE FLOW

The **Gulf Stream** is a strong **current** in the Atlantic Ocean. It is fast and warm. It always takes the same path. Many animals ride the Gulf Stream.

The Gulf Stream starts in the Gulf of Mexico. Then it moves up the east coast of North America and turns toward Europe.

A SEA IN AN OCEAN

The **Sargasso Sea** is in the Atlantic Ocean. Currents go in a circle around it. They set the sea apart from the rest of the Atlantic Ocean. Seaweed grows here. Baby turtles and eels often grow up here. It is shelter for many animals.

The Sargasso Sea is the world's only sea inside an ocean.

The Sargasso Sea is named for sargassum, the seaweed that floats there.

Most North Atlantic
hurricanes form from
June to November.

STORMY WEATHER

Hurricanes are big storms. They form over warm water near the **equator**. Hurricanes have strong winds. Sometimes they reach land. They bring rain, floods, and dangerous winds.

The doldrums is an area in the Atlantic and Pacific Oceans with very little wind. The doldrums is near the equator.

LOOKING COOL

Look out! Icebergs are huge chunks of ice. They float in the ocean. The North Atlantic has many icebergs. They are a danger to ships.

Icebergs that show less than 16 feet (5 m) above the water are called bergy bits. Even smaller icebergs are called growlers.

Icebergs travel with ocean currents.

The Mid-Atlantic Ridge is part of the longest mountain range on Earth.

ISLANDS CAN BE MOUNTAINTOPS

What's that in the water? Is it an island? A mountain? It's both! It's the **Mid-Atlantic Ridge**. A ridge is a line of mountains. Most of these mountains are under water. The tops of the tallest mountains are islands.

The Azores are islands near Portugal. They are part of the Mid-Atlantic Ridge.

DEEPEST POINT

The Atlantic Ocean's deepest point is called the Milwaukee Deep. It is near Puerto Rico. The Milwaukee Deep is more than 5 miles (8 km) deep.

The Milwaukee Deep is named after the ship that discovered it.

Modern machines can travel into parts of the Milwaukee Deep.

Mako sharks live in warm Atlantic waters.

A HEALTHY OCEAN

Many animals call the Atlantic Ocean home. Whales and dolphins live here. So do birds, seals, and turtles. Sharks and many other types of fish live in the Atlantic Ocean, too.

Many Atlantic fish and whales feed on plankton. Plankton are tiny creatures that float in the water.

A GOOD HOME

The Atlantic Ocean can be many things. It is big. It is surprising. It is full of danger. It is a good home. Many animals depend on the Atlantic Ocean. People do, too. Let's take good care of it!

The Atlantic Ocean was named by the ancient Greeks. It means "Sea of Atlas."

The Atlantic Ocean is more than 10 times larger than the United States.

GLOSSARY

current (KUR-rent): A current is a flow of water in a river or ocean. In the ocean, a current always takes the same basic path.

equator (ee-KWAY-tur): The equator is the imaginary line that runs around the middle of Earth. The equator is halfway between the North Pole and the South Pole. Waters near the equator are always warm.

Gulf Stream (GULF STREEM): The Gulf Stream is a warm, strong current in the Atlantic Ocean. The Gulf Stream starts in the Gulf of Mexico, then it moves up the east coast of North America and turns toward Europe.

hurricane (HUR-uh-kayn): A hurricane is a large, swirling storm that forms over warm water at the equator. Hurricanes usually travel north, northeast, or east.

Mid-Atlantic Ridge (MID-at-LAN-tik RIJ): The Mid-Atlantic Ridge is an underwater mountain range that runs down the middle of the Atlantic Ocean. It is part of the longest mountain range on Earth.

Sargasso Sea (sar-GAS-so SEE): The Sargasso Sea is an area of the North Atlantic Ocean that is protected by the currents that circle around it. The sea is named after sargassum, a seaweed that floats there.

TO FIND OUT MORE

Books

Oachs, Emily Rose. *Atlantic Ocean*. Minneapolis, MN: Bellwether Media. 2016.

Spilsbury, Louise, and Richard Spilsbury. *Atlantic Ocean*. Chicago, IL: Heinemann Raintree, 2015.

Wilsdon, Christina. *Ultimate Oceanpedia: The Most Complete Ocean Reference Ever*. Washington, DC: National Geographic Children's Books, 2016.

Woodward, John. *Ocean: A Visual Encyclopedia*. New York, NY: DK Publishing, 2015.

Web Sites

Visit our Web site for links about the Atlantic Ocean:

childsworld.com/links

Note to Parents, Teachers, and Librarians: We routinely verify our Web links to make sure they are safe and active sites. So encourage your readers to check them out!

INDEX

ABOUT THE AUTHOR

Juniata Rogers grew up in Newport, RI, an island town on the Atlantic Ocean. She has worked as a naturalist, an art model, and a teacher. She's been writing professionally for 25 years, and currently lives near Washington, DC.